Garage Sale Fever!

GARAGE SALE
fever!

By John D. Schroeder

DeForest Press
Elk River, Minnesota

Published by:
DeForest Press
P.O. Box 154
Elk River, MN 55330 USA
www.DeForestPress.com
Toll-free: 877-441-9733
Richard DeForest Erickson, Publisher
Shane Groth, Editor in Chief

Cover design by Linda Walters, Optima Graphics, Appleton, WI

ISBN 1-930374-16-X

Printed in the United States of America
09 08 07 06 05   5 4 3 2 1

Dedicated to my Fab Four:

Barbara J. Winter
Georgia Pergakis
Shane Groth
David A. Anderson

In appreciation for their encouragement & advice

Contents

Introduction

I caught garage sale fever over three decades ago. I had all the symptoms: the anticipation of the spring garage sale season, the thrill of the hunt, the joy from having perfect strangers hand over money for my stuff, the urge to buy used instead of paying retail, the need to own a station wagon, having difficulty driving past a sale without stopping, and not wanting the season to end in the fall. I am hooked on rummage.

And this is a good thing! Throughout my travels I have encountered wonderful people (some not), been able to view the unwanted trash and treasure of thousands of sellers, added to my various collections, and learned the rules and techniques of garage sale commerce. I have received quite an education.

As a writer with a passion for garage sales and flea markets, this book is the next logical step of my journey. I have the desire to share my stories and my ideas for garage sale success with others who have the Fever.

Although I strongly believe that plain dumb luck plays a major role in garage sale endeavors for both buyers and sellers, I also know it is more than being at the right place at the right time. There are skills required for both buyers and sellers. And you gain these skills by experience, learning from mistakes, and listening to others. It is a continuing education.

Although I confess to being a garage sale junkie, I also have a regular life. I make my living as a full time writer and copy editor, working out of my home. Writing pays my bills. I am not a dealer of collectibles. I buy more than I sell and I sell only a few times a year only to make room to buy more. I buy to add to my collections. When I am not working, I frequent garage sales and flea markets. If you have the Fever, you know what I mean.

One aspect of this book that makes it unique is that it contains stories. Through my travels in Garage Sale Land I have discovered that everybody has a garage sale story. If you listen to others at garage sales and flea markets you hear stories of the treasure that got away or the one that didn't. This book shares some of my experiences including the time I had to call 911 during my lawn sale, the time I chased a bicycle thief, and the VCR that held a hidden surprise. These stories, along with those that tell about the treasures I discovered, are part of me as much as they are a part of everyone who has ever rejoiced over a garage sale find. We all have our stories.

Introduction

It is my hope that this book contains both stories that will inspire you to continue your quest for treasure and ideas that will make you more effective as a buyer or seller. I am sincerely passing along to you the best of my years of experience. Whether you are a garage sale novice or pro, there is always more to learn. If you have the Fever, the only cure is to experience for yourself the world of trash and treasure. Enjoy the journey.

Ten Reasons I Love Garage Sales!

1. You never know what treasure you will discover.
2. You can sit at a table in your garage and strangers hand you money all day.
3. You can earn extra income without leaving your home.
4. It's an opportunity to get cash for stuff you no longer need or want.
5. You meet all kinds of interesting people.
6. You learn about luck and being at the right place at the right time.
7. You can often buy things at very low prices. Why pay retail?
8. Whatever you collect, you can find it at garage sales, often at bargain prices.
9. You can always make an offer instead of paying the asking price.
10. Holding a yard sale is usually a good way to make it rain.

Selling Ideas

Making the Best of Your Location

Location, location, location. It's important for any retail business and the same holds true for your garage sale. The location of your sale does play a role in the potential success of your sale. Although you probably did not make the decision to buy or rent your home by considering whether or not it would be a good location for a garage sale, some people do live in great spots for holding a sale, while others do not. The trick is to make the best of what you have.

The ideal location for a garage or lawn sale is facing a busy or fairly busy street that allows parking in front of your residence. This situation is perfect for a lawn sale. It is also excellent for a garage sale IF your driveway runs along the side of your home and intersects with that busy street. In either situation, this allows you to display your rummage in view of those driving down your street. You either fill your lawn, driveway or garage with the items you are selling.

Your customers just need to park in front and get out of their cars. You don't need to advertise or put up signs. It's evident you are having a garage sale.

The next ideal location is the same as above, with the problem that no parking is allowed in front of your home. People passing by in cars can see your sale, but they can't pull over to the curb and park. If this is your situation, I would use signs pointing to where cars can park, usually around the corner from your home. A sign could also encourage parking in your driveway, although this has space limitations.

If your garage is located in an alley, this is a good location, but not the best. You need to use your creativity to get people to drive down your alley or park at the end of the alley and walk. Start with a big sign in your front yard or on top of your car parked in front of your home saying "Garage Sale Today in Alley". Banners or balloons are effective ways to get attention, both in your front yard and in the alley. Place a garage sale sign with arrows at the entrance to your alley. Attach a balloon to it. Another smart idea is to string a banner across the alley where your garage is so when people look down the alley, they will see your location. Some people will walk down the alley; others will drive. For an extra boost, advertise your sale in your local newspaper.

If you are like my parents, you live in the suburbs and there is little traffic on your street. The busy street is two blocks down. First, advertise your sale in the newspaper. It's a must. Second, place a large garage sale sign on your corner next to the busy street. Attach a balloon to the sign. Include an arrow on the sign and your address in big letters. Maybe have a companion sign saying "First Day Garage Sale." Even better, talk a neighbor into having their garage sale the same day and your sign can read "Multiple Garage Sales" or "Neighborhood Sale" with the appropriate directional arrow.

Have a real bad location and want to have a garage sale real bad? I might consider packing up all the rummage and moving it to the front lawn or garage of a friend or relative who live in a good location. Ask nicely. And maybe they have some stuff to sell, too!

Another idea, related to the idea above, is that if you know the Kingfield Neighborhood holds their giant garage sale every year the second weekend in May, go to that neighborhood and "rent" a front yard or driveway for the day from someone not participating in the community sale. Better yet, try to find someone you actually know who lives in the Kingfield neighborhood or do the "friend of a friend" thing. Use some contacts from friends or relatives.

Live in an apartment building, condo, or in a townhouse? Organize a resident's lawn or garage sale with your neighbors. Be sure to follow any rules that exist from management or your complex. Advertise if you are not in a high traffic area. You might even be able to have the sale in a community room.

Make the best of your location by using some creativity and advance planning. You can have a garage or lawn sale almost anywhere. All you need to do is make the most of the strengths of the location and compensate for any weaknesses. Good luck!

Selling Ideas
Before the Sale

IDEA: Start preparing for your sale at least a week in advance.

Try doing a little bit each day for seven days before your sale. Price items during the week so you can focus on setting up the day of or the day before the sale. Get some quarters and dollar bills from the bank so you can make change. Put someone to work making signs. The more you do early and delegate to others, the easier things will go.

IDEA: Get your friends and neighbors to add their items to your sale. Go for volume!

The more items you have out and visible to cars and people passing by, the greater the chance there is that people may stop at your sale. A front lawn or a garage that is packed with all kinds of merchandise is a major drawing card. Think of it this way: Would you be more likely to stop at a sale that features a card table with 10 items, or one that is packed with more items that you can count? In order to sell, you need people to stop. It's as simple as that. Have friends and neighbors price and tag their items so you can easily keep track. Another strategy is to invite neighbors to hold a sale the same day as your sale.

IDEA: Put a price on each item.

Use pricing stickers to price each item you want to sell. This idea has several benefits. One is that it encourages you to think about pricing rather than making it up as you go along. Another reason for pricing is that you won't have ten people coming up to you at once each holding a different item and asking "How much is this?" The question gets tiring after a while. Also, sometimes when people see an unpriced item, they may pass it by thinking it costs too much, or they may just not want to bother you to ask about it. Pricing is the first step toward selling.

IDEA: Test items that use electricity before the sale to see whether they work or not. State on the tag is the item works or if it is broken.

It only takes a minute to plug in that old toaster, radio or clock to see if it runs. If it works, you can price it accordingly with a clean conscience. If it is broken, mark it as such, lower the price, and someone still may buy it. Many times if items are not marked as working, people will assume they are broken without inquiring about it. Testing items before the sale will also save you from taking time out during the sale to plug in items to see if they work in response to customer questions.

IDEA: Clean your items.

People are more likely to buy items that are clean and appear to be well cared for, rather than those that are dirty and dusty. Clothes, glassware and dishes are especially important to clean. Dust off bikes, chairs, tables and furniture.

IDEA: Create an instant display case.

Have some small items that need protection, but you don't have a display case? Use a small drawer and use duct tape to secure clear glass or clear plastic to one side of the drawer so the glass or plastic can be lifted up. Cover the bottom of the drawer with nice cloth. Put a sign on the glass or plastic—ask for assistance. Place your new display case near your cashier / checkout table, so someone can keep an eye on it. HINT—Keep an eye out for wooden drawers thrown out as trash. They not only make good display cases, they are often better than boxes for displaying and carrying items. Drawers are quick and easy displays for video tapes and books.

IDEA: Before the sale, search your home for things

you don't need or don't use.

You'll be amazed at all the stuff in your home that you don't need, don't use and can easily do without. If you haven't used something in 3 years, put it in the sale. Clean out closets, go through the basement, and maybe get rid of some of those books you have and haven't read. Make a game of seeing how much stuff you can find for your sale. Get rid of it now, instead of later, and get some cash instead!

IDEA: Eliminate all hazards from the sale area so your customers don't get hurt on anything.

In this age of lawsuits it is wise to protect yourself. Make sure there is nothing to trip over like cords or boxes. Don't leave sharp objects around. Put safety tape on steps so people can see whether to step up or step down. If there are low spots or holes in your lawn, fill them up or place something over them so no one falls. Do a safety evaluation before your sale begins.

IDEA: Sell a variety of items, something for everyone.

There is no law against selling just children's clothes, and many people may be looking for them, but you really restrict your potential customers if you limit what you sell. A variety of items will bring you a larger and diverse crowd of people. Try to sell items that appeal to men and women of all ages. Again, the more items you have out, the better your sale will be.

IDEA: Increase your table space by placing plywood boards between tables.

By placing a sturdy plywood board between two card tables that are a few feet apart, you increase your display space. Large empty boxes placed on their side or upside down can also be utilized to place items upon.

Use plywood between tables to increase selling space.

IDEA: If you want to sell a tent, put the tent up.

If someone is in the market for a tent and drives by your sale, they won't see your tent if it is sitting in a box or a bag. Take some time to assemble the tent and you'll have a much better chance of selling it.

IDEA: Don't sell in the dark. Have a light or lamps in your garage.

It is difficult for people to buy things from you if they can't see what you have for sale. If your garage does not have electricity, run an extension cord from the house. Having several lamps on tables within your garage also brightens things up. A well-lit garage also prevents accidents.

IDEA: Decide in advance what to do about people who want to purchase items before your sale opens.

If you place a classified ad in the newspaper listing what you are selling, chances are antique dealers and avid garage salers may pay you a visit the night before your sale opens wanting to view your rummage. Dealers will purchase what you have priced too low and re-sell it. If you don't mind this and just want to sell stuff, let them in. If you want everyone to have an equal chance when the sale opens, use the words "No pre-sales" in your ad and maybe also post it outside your garage.

IDEA: Put live batteries in items that require them.

You'll increase your chances of making a sale if the item you are selling is operational. People are hesitant to buy an item that may or may not work, based on the word of a stranger. Add the cost of the batteries to your sale price.

IDEA: Prepare for rain.

Even if there is not a cloud in the sky when you begin your sale in the morning, consider the possibility of a downpour. If it gets cloudy, turn the radio on. If it looks like rain, act to protect valuable items. Have plastic handy to cover items that are outdoors.

IDEA: Do not damage items by using masking tape for price tags.
If you write a price on a piece of masking tape and place it on a book, puzzle or an old magazine that may be collectible, the item may be damaged when the buyer attempts to remove the sticker and ends up ripping the paper off the item. Masking tape can also be hard to remove from plastic items. In short, don't use masking tape for pricing. Use white stickers for pricing and test them before hand to see that they peel off without tearing.

If you are selling drinking glasses and mugs, they should be clean and free of chips.

IDEA: Decide in advance whether or not you will accept checks. Post your decision for people to see.
You may want to limit your acceptance of checks to only those in your area or neighborhood. Remember you can also direct people to the nearest Automatic

Teller Machine (ATM) if you will only accept cash.

IDEA: Prepare for wind.

Strong winds and gusts can be just as damaging as rain. Remove shades from lamps so they can't easily be toppled by wind. Fasten down light objects such as magazines and papers. Place pictures and art framed in glass in protected areas.

Selling Ideas: Promoting Your Sale

IDEA: If you live on a busy street, slow down traffic by parking a car in front of your house.

If your sale is in view of a busy street (as opposed to being in an alley), don't let traffic speed by your sale. Parking a car in front may get them to slow down and take a look, or even stop. Put a sign on top of your car for extra advertising. Several cars parked in front (neighbors, friends) can make your sale appear busier than it is. (Would you be more likely to stop at a sale that appears to be packed with people, or one that has few customers?)

IDEA: Signs that promote your sale should be brief, specific and use large print.

You are better off using stand-alone signs that are stuck into the ground rather than taping one to a telephone pole that is cluttered with signs, many for sales that were weeks ago. Print large. Don't just use an arrow—always include an address. Be specific—instead of just "Thursday," write "Thursday, June 12." You may want to list a few items you are selling, but keep it brief.

IDEA: Draw attention to your sale using three-dimensional banners.

Colorful, moving items help draw attention to your sale. In addition to balloons, try a string of flags, banners, windsocks, giant seasonal decorations (for example, inflatable Christmas or Easter figures), or the American flag. These will help slow down passersby and encourage them to stop.

Use 3-D items, like a string of flags, to help draw customers.

IDEA: Give good directions to your sale.

A sign on the corner saying "Garage Sale" with an arrow pointing toward your home or garage can leave people guessing as to the location of the sale. Put your address on the sign (even in small print) and date it, including hours of the sale. Attaching a balloon to it will help it get noticed. Do use an arrow on your sign. Multiple signs in various locations will draw more customers. Also—and this is important—remember to check during the sale that the signs are still up and have not fallen over or been removed.

IDEA: Advertise number of participants.

If you and four other people are joining together to have a sale, advertise it on signs as "Five Family Sale." Potential customers are attracted to larger sales with multiple sellers.

IDEA: Try truth in advertising.

Don't use the words "HUGE SALE" on your sign if your sale has only a dozen items. Skip the word "huge." It is used so often it means nothing. You are better off using words like "Antiques" or "Children's Clothes," promoting what you are selling rather than the size of the sale.

IDEA: Network with other garage sales in your area.

If there is another garage sale going on nearby during your sale, direct your customers to it, and request that the other sale return the favor. Signs or flyers can be used. This is often a win-win situation for all concerned.

IDEA: If you post signs on telephone poles, take them down when your sale is over.

Help keep your neighborhood attractive by removing your signs after your sale. Keep a list of locations where they were posted and then it will just take minutes to rip them down.

Selling Ideas During the Sale

IDEA: Put a "hot" item where people can see it for the purpose of stopping traffic.

For example, I've used a 1940s floor model radio to get people to stop at my lawn sales. Most furniture (tables, wood chairs) works well also. The most unusual (and best) traffic stopper I ever used was a seven-foot full color cardboard cutout of a smiling young man wearing only a towel (from a beer advertisement). I propped it up against a tree and it did get people to notice and to stop at my sale. Unusual and in demand items often can get people out of their car to check the price—and then they may look at other merchandise. I put the biggest and best stuff close to the curb where people will see it. You want an item or items that will get drivers to stop and get out of their cars. Use your creativity.

IDEA: Be friendly. Greet your shoppers.

Make a point to try and talk to those who visit your sale. A smile and good eye contact is good for business. A brief greeting on your part may break the ice and open them up to ask questions about a particular item you have. Make your prospects feel welcome.

IDEA: Rearrange your items as the sale continues so your displays remain attractive.

How you display what you have for sale is critical to your success. As items sell, move other items into their place so people just arriving at your sale will view a full display and not a lot of open space and leftovers. Make your items look attractive and have them easy to view.

Virtually everything sells eventually.

IDEA: Have a FREE PILE, a designated area of items that you are giving away at no cost.

Put a giant "FREE" sign next to a dozen or so items you just want to get rid of and watch the stuff disappear! (I've given away broken bikes, old chairs, books, records and glassware just to clean out the clutter). Having a "free box" containing smaller items is good also, but bigger items get people to stop at your sale. Often if people take a free item they also feel the need to purchase something from you. The purpose of giving things away, however, is to move items out of your life. This is a better alternative than to put items out for trash collection.

IDEA: Keep small items and valuables near you or under glass.

Shoplifting is not limited to retail stores. You need to protect yourself and keep alert. Watch your valuables. Be careful of small items like rings, watches, jewelry, coins, stamps, etc. Use a glass covered display case if possible.

IDEA: Keep your money safe.

Retailers always use security measures with their money and so should you. Don't leave your money alone and unguarded. Keep it with you in a pocket or wallet, lock it in a drawer, and regularly bring larger bills into the safety of your home.

IDEA: Keep your house locked during the sale.

Whether you are having your sale in your yard or garage, keep the doors to the house locked. With people roaming all over, it's too easy for someone to slip inside and steal something.

IDEA: Encourage people to make an offer if they

see something they are interested in.

Some people may be hesitant to make an offer on one of the many treasures you are offering, so encourage them by having a few signs saying "Offers Considered" or tell them verbally. Many people will need no encouragement to submit an offer.

IDEA: Display books on blankets.

Hardcover and paperback books can be displayed face-up on blankets on your lawn, making them easy for your customers to see the full cover rather than just the side. If your lawn has a slight incline or hill, this works even better.

IDEA: Have photographs or notices of large items that are not on display at your sale.

If your neighbor has a refrigerator for sale, or your cousin is selling a dining room set, have them take a photo of it and then prominently display the photo at your sale. If a photo is not available, a large printed notice may generate some prospects.

IDEA: Put your stuff ON tables, not UNDER them.

Not all people are going to take the time to look under a table for additional items, so you may lose some sales by leaving items underneath tables. What's especially a bad idea is leaving things inside boxes under a table. If you don't have enough table space, borrow a card table from a neighbor. Another alternative is to display items on a blanket or rug. Try to have everything out in the open where it can easily be seen (and sold)!

IDEA: Have a box of 25 cents each items; 50 cents each, and so on.

You'll find that the majority of your sales will come from these items. People love to dig through boxes looking for bargains. Pack some boxes full of cheap treasures. They don't need to be individually priced. This is also a good opportunity to rid your home of all those little things you never use.

IDEA: Have a box of giveaway items for kids.

It is a way to keep children occupied and distracted from handling expensive or breakable items. Sometimes it is a solution for parents whose kids keep saying, "Buy me something." Items may include children's books, crayons, toys, etc. Have the parent select an appropriate choice for their child.

IDEA: Promote other opportunities.

Give your customers business cards and handouts. If your spouse operates a car repair service, give each visitor to your sale a business card. If your church is looking for new members or has a special event to promote, drop a flyer into each bag of rummage you sell. If you are a collector of some specific item, put what you are looking for on a flyer or card to hand out or drop in a bag.

IDEA: Don't cut prices until the afternoon.

Wait a while before you begin accepting offers. By the afternoon you will know what items have generated interest and may sell, and which items you may need to cut in price if you want to sell them. Remember you always have the option to counter an offer.

IDEA: Be good to yourself.

Having a garage sale should be fun and profitable, so enjoy the experience. Be sure you have enough help at your sale, especially for set-up and take-down. Have a comfortable chair to sit in—get off your feet and rest when you can. Have some food or snacks handy. Have a book to read if things get slow.

IDEA: Remove money from your house at night.

If someone thinks you have a large amount of money in your home after a sale, you are asking for trouble. Lock the money in the trunk of your car or give it to a relative for safe keeping until you can deposit it in the bank.

One Hot Selling Idea: Instant Ancestors

Interested in a high profit item that you can easily create and sell repeatedly? Then gather together all those empty picture frames you have around the house and locate some vintage photographs to put inside them.

Let me share with you my discovery. Over the years, I had accumulated literally hundreds of photos that ended up tossed together loose in boxes. Some came from my grandparents' estate. Others I had purchased by the box at garage sales. Few had any identification. I really did not want them any more, but I didn't want to destroy them, so I pondered how I could put them to good use.

About the same time I happened to notice that practically every sale I went to had empty picture frames for sale. And most of the time they were dirt

Clayton

cheap, 25 or 50 cents each. I also observed that empty frames were not really big sellers. Usually, if people want an empty frame, they will buy the exact size they need at a discount store and not search garage sales for them. This gave me an idea.

What I did was take some of my best and most

interesting vintage photographs and I started putting them in attractive frames that I purchased at garage sales. My concept was to sell framed vintage photos as art. Think about it: They are one of a kind, usually at least 70 years old, and can be just as attractive as a painting when displayed on a wall or desk. And they are great as conversation pieces!

My friends call my creations "instant ancestors" as they have the potential to become immediate members of the family tree, related by a garage sale purchase, rather than by blood. If you don't have photos of past generations, this is the chance to remedy the situation. And you could give the people pictured any name you want!

As an experiment, I put together about a dozen framed photos and displayed them on a table at my garage sale. The response was amazing. People

immediately started buying them at five to ten dollars each. One woman spent thirty dollars! The vintage photos generated much conversation and speculation. People crowded around the table to view them. They attracted all types of buyers, even some construction workers who stopped by. My customers saw them as inexpensive original art for their desks, tables and walls at home. My "photo art" sold well at two lawn sales and at two flea markets that year.

There was the 1930s framed photograph of a young girl pushing a baby carriage with her pet bulldog nearby. Photographs of vintage cars were popular. Beach scenes with men in one-piece bathing suits were in demand. Portraits of men and women wearing the latest in 1920s fashions sold well. People liked vintage sports photos (especially golfers and football players), along with photos of old homes and carriages pulled by horses.

Attractively framed vintage photos do sell well as original art. And I believe the photos are so well received because they are nicely framed. Framed photos are ready to display on a wall or desk. The buyer doesn't have to hunt around for a frame. Just like buying a painting, they know the exact place they want to display it.

Try it out. Select some photos from the 1940s or earlier and match them with a nice wood or metal frame. Photos of babies, dogs and cars sell well. It is better if a

Writing on the back of this photo begins,
"Taken December 5, 1917. This is just
another rotten picture of me..."

person appears in the photo. Be sure the vintage photo is sharp, preferably a close up of the subject. Charge five dollars and up, depending on the size and quality. If it is a photograph that you personally like and one that generates attention, it's a good candidate for an instant ancestor.

Advice for Selling at Flea Markets

If you want to reach a large pool of buyers for your rummage and collectibles, perhaps renting a table or a space at a flea market is for you. The cost for a flea market space ranges from $15 and up. At larger flea markets you may pay several hundred dollars for a space. You furnish your own tables for displaying your merchandise and need to bring along most of the ingredients needed for a garage sale: start-up money, bags, and so on. Spaces are assigned on a first come, first served basis.

Chances are you have attended a flea market and know what they are like. To get a better feel for it, I would encourage you to talk to someone who has sold items at the flea market you are considering. Ask some questions about sales volume and attendance.

Some flea markets are Saturday to Sunday events

while others are one day or evening events. Others are Sunday morning only, 6 A.M. to noon. Many metropolitan areas offer several flea markets a year, some monthly, and some even weekly. In northern climates, the flea market season is the same as the garage sale season, May through October. Do some research and select the flea market that is right for you.

You can sell just about anything at the flea market. Many people sell homemade crafts. You will find anything and everything that can be found at a garage sale. People sell collectibles, VCRs, DVDs, videos, television sets, CD players, CDs, records, books, clothing, art, tires, tools, computers, cameras—you name it, and you can probably find it. Some sellers have a bit of everything, while others specialize with maybe just railroad memorabilia, or fruits and vegetables.

Some of the larger flea markets allow you to set up your tables and wares the day before the sale. You may have to camp out and provide overnight security for your stuff. At most flea markets the sellers show up and set up in the early morning hours, 4 A.M. to 6 A.M. Customers will often show up about the same time. In order to pull this off, you need to select and carefully pack your items in your car or van the day before and then leave home in enough time to begin setting up in the early morning hours.

Flea markets can attract hundreds if not thousands of potential buyers. But unlike your own garage sale, you are competing with other sellers. While at your garage sale a customer might leisurely browse, at a flea market your table may only get a quick walk-by because there is so much for people to see.

HINT: have an unusual item prominently on display to slow people down. The weather is another factor. Flea markets can be rained out. You go through all the work and then a downpour starts at 8 A.M. Customers flee and you struggle to quickly cover up your rummage. Always bring along sheets of plastic in case it rains.

If you do decide to sell at a flea market, how you display your items is critical. Attractively display your merchandise. Make them easy to see. Create a good flow of foot traffic in the area of your booth. Make it inviting to come in and easy to exit. Put your best items (or the stuff you really want to sell) up front and close to people who pass by. And it is very important to chat with those who look at your items or those who are passing by. You need to be an attentive and considerate sales person. Start up a conversation about the antique clock or trumpet a person is carrying with them.

Selling at a flea market is hard work, but it can be financially rewarding with planning and a little luck. Maybe this is your year to give flea markets a try!

Buying Ideas

Buying Ideas

IDEA: The early bird gets the worm. Begin as early as possible.

Garage sales generally begin between 8 A.M. and 9 A.M. mostly on Thursdays, Fridays, and Saturdays. Be aware of people just opening or in the process of setting up—hang around so you can be first to check out their stuff. If you are going to an estate sale early, plan to take a number and to wait in line. Prime time for estate sales is 8 A.M. to noon, but sales continue into the afternoon.

IDEA: Plan your route and strategy before you leave home.

Scan the garage sale classifieds for sales of interest to you, also noting any estate sales in the same area. Make a list of addresses you wish to check out. Use an index card to plan a route. This will save time and gas. Unadvertised sales you find along the way are a bonus. Hint: Get cash the day before so you don't have to stop at a bank or an ATM.

IDEA: Bring along a list of your needs.

Take a look around your house and list the items you need that could be purchased at a garage sale rather than paying full price at a retail store. Are you looking for specific books? Need tools or a new lawn sprinkler. How about an extension cord? By creating a list, it may jog your memory when you see the item at a sale. Think of it as a scavenger hunt!

IDEA: Pay for your purchase with the lowest denominator of bill.

Many sellers do not have a lot of change on hand, so try to pay for your purchases with small bills and change closest to the total you owe. You can pay for a 25 cent purchase with a twenty dollar bill at a retail store, but that can really put a strain on available funds at a garage sale. Try carrying lots of small bills and change on your garage sale adventures to help the sellers out.

IDEA: Inspect items carefully for cracks, chips and defects.

Let the buyer beware is especially appropriate at garage sales. You can get a bargain or a worthless piece of junk—for the same price. The best advice is to be cautious. Check items over carefully to see if there is anything wrong with them. Some sellers will put "as is" on the price tag which is a clue something is wrong. In glassware and dishes, chips and cracks will drastically reduce the value of an item, so be especially careful there. Look for stains on cloth items and clothing. Once you buy it, you can't return it, so if it looks too good to be true, beware!

IDEA: If you don't see it, ask.

It never hurts to ask if you don't see an item you are looking to buy. If there are dozens of things on tables, the item you want may be there is plain view. It could also be in the bottom of a box under the table, or still inside the house. Ask and you may find!

IDEA: Plug in items that require electricity prior to purchasing them.

Most sellers will be happy to point you toward an electrical outlet so you can see how well something runs before you buy it. If you gamble and buy it without testing it and find it does not work, you are generally stuck with it as garage sale purchases are usually final. Rarely are return privileges extended.

IDEA: Feel free to make an offer.

Most of the time people don't mind if you make an offer on something you are interested in. Your offer could be up to half of the listed price, but don't press your luck. For example, on a five dollar item, offering three or four dollars is often considered reasonable. If the sale has been going on all day, the chances are better of your offer being accepted. Don't make an offer unless you intend to buy it at that price. Your offer might also be met with a counter offer.

IDEA: Lock your car and put all valuables in the trunk when you go to a garage sale or an estate sale.

It doesn't take long for someone to open a car door and grab belongings that are sitting in the back seat of your car. If you are going to sales in a poor area of town or in an unfamiliar neighborhood, locking your car can also prevent armed robbery or carjacking.

IDEA: Inspect clothing carefully.

When buying clothes at sales, you can get bargains or you can get taken. Be on the lookout for stains. Be sure clothing will fit you or a member of your family. Check labels and washing instructions.

IDEA: If you are purchasing multiple items, be sure you receive them all.

It occasionally happens in stores where you buy a lot of items and when you get home some are missing. The same is true with garage sales. Usually it has nothing to do with dishonesty. What happens is the seller is in a hurry because other buyers are waiting and one or more items don't make it into your bag of purchases. Watch carefully when items are packed in bags so you get everything you purchased.

IDEA: Keep track of your purchases. Carry a pen and notebook with you in your car.
There are several good reasons to record all your purchases in writing. It will show you how much you are spending each week. You will know where your money is going. If you decide to sell items later, you will know how much you paid for them. Your garage sale notebook can also contain jottings about items you have seen, prices and addresses, even your car mileage.

IDEA: If you are thinking about buying an item, write down the address so you can go back.
It is easy to get lost in unfamiliar neighborhoods. You may think you know exactly where you saw that lawn mower or bicycle, but once you drive on to ten more sales, you may have difficulty locating a previous sale even one half hour later. It takes just a few moments to jot down an address. It can be a good investment of time on your part.

IDEA: Take along a list of the needs of others.
As long as you are out and about, keep your

eyes open for that lawn mower your father needs, the antique birdhouse you could give a friend for a birthday present, or the computer software your neighbor has been after. Keep an eye out for collectibles. Chances are many of your friends or family members may collect items you may come across, like plates, old knives, purses, key chains or radios. You can help someone add to his or her collection often at bargain prices. Be sure of price range and repayment before you do this. If you see something, you can also get the telephone number of the seller and give it to your collecting friend. Collectibles you pick up at sales during the year can also be saved for birthday and Christmas gifts.

Keep a city map and a map of neighborhoods in your car. It can save you time and gasoline if you know where you are and where you are going.

IDEA: Take advantage of bag sales when available at the end of estate sales and church rummage sales.

In order to sell remaining rummage, some church and estate sales will have bag sales just prior to closing. They will give you a large brown grocery bag for several dollars and let you fill it with the rummage that remains. Some restrictions may apply. You can usually mix books, clothes, glassware—anything that fits within the bag. You can be surprised often at what is left over, frequently because it was overpriced, too common, or odd. And yes, treasures are some times overlooked!

IDEA: If the seller doesn't know if the item works, assume it does not work.

You will be rarely disappointed. If you know how to repair things, garage sales offer wonderful opportunities for handy and resourceful people. You will find many broken items at garage sales. Again, try to plug in electrical items and test them. Once in a great while you will be surprised as a "broken" item will work.

IDEA: The second best time to go to a garage sale is right at closing time.

If you can't be there when a sale starts, be there when it ends. Frequently some great stuff at great prices remain only because the right buyer did not stop at the sale. Items also remain if the sale was not well attended. Closing time is also great for negotiating lower prices from sellers who do not want to pack things up. Bargains are also plentiful at flea markets when vendors are packing up.

IDEA: Dress for garage sale success.

Dress in layers when you start out during the cool morning hours so you can shed clothes as it gets warmer. Comfortable shoes are also vital. You do a lot more walking than you realize and you will feel it at the end of the day. Carry an umbrella in the car in case of rain.

IDEA: At neighborhood sales, ask for a map of sales.

Many well-organized neighborhood sales will have maps available of all homes that are participating that day. Once you get a map, cross out places you have been to and pay attention to isolated sales at the edge of a neighborhood that may get less traffic. Some maps also include a list of rummage at various locations.

IDEA: If you are a collector, bring along and distribute business cards containing your name, phone number and hobby.

You never know who you will run into at a sale. A conversation with a seller may result in a valuable contact—a person who has just the item you are looking for to add to your collection. Make it a practice of starting conversations with sellers and let them know what you collect. And leave a way for them to contact you.

IDEA: If you drive down an alley to get to a garage sale, don't leave your car in the middle of the alley blocking traffic.

You can save time by driving down an alley to see if a garage sale is worth stopping at, but if you park your vehicle, have some consideration for others and do not block the alley with your car. Pull your car or truck into a nearby driveway so other cars can pass by. Just as much as you dislike being blocked in an alley, don't block the alley for others.

IDEA: If you are a collector, remember to bring along a price reference guide for the items you collect.

Many antique malls carry reference guides for most every sort of collectible. Don't leave your guide at home. Throw it in the backseat of your car for quick reference. You never know when you will come across a treasure and need to know the price of an item. Keep the reference guide in your car all summer long.

IDEA: Look for underpriced items made in the 1930s through the 1960s.

These items may be collectibles and either a dealer or a collector might pay you big money for your discovery. If an item is old, in good condition, and reasonably priced, you may want to make the investment. Visit an antique mall to get an idea of prices.

IDEA: If you are considering buying an item, don't set it back down until you decide you are not going to buy it.

This rule you often learn the hard way. You pick up an item, look at it, set it back down, then someone else picks it up and buys it. Even if there is no one in sight, do not set the item down and walk away. It could be in the hands of another person in less than a minute. Carry the item around with you if you are undecided or ask the seller to put it on hold for you for a few minutes.

IDEA: Multiply your efforts by having friends and family members search garage sales for you.

If there is something you collect or really need for your house, have other people be on the lookout. You can't be at all sales, so have a friend keep watch in his or her neighborhood while you do the same in your area. If you are going to a neighborhood sale together, you might want to split the area in half and meet back at the car in a half hour. It can pay big dividends to have many pairs of eyes wide open during the garage sale season.

IDEA: Beware of antique reproductions. If in doubt, ask the seller the age of the item.

It can be difficult at times to tell if an item is old or new. Don't assume it is old if it looks old. Ask.

Buying Ideas

Sometimes you may be lucky enough to hear the family history of an antique and be able to learn more about the item you wish to purchase.

Different Types of Sales

- Garage sales and lawn sales—usually in the spring, summer and fall.
- Estate sales—a sale of belongings inside a house in multiple rooms. It usually means someone has died or gone to a nursing home.
- Moving sales—held inside a house or a garage, usually after a house has been sold, but sometimes before the house goes on the market or while it is on the market.
- Neighborhood sales—multiple garage and lawn sales within the same area. Quite often advertised in newspapers. Crowded with buyers. Go early—you may have trouble parking.
- Church rummage sales—a single location with many contributors, usually lasting for several days. Admission may be charged on first day.
- Alley sales—a group of garage sales in an alley.
- Block sales—a mixture of garage and front lawn sales, usually limited to one or two residential blocks.
- Apartment sale—where one or more parties set up tables outside of an apartment building.
- Flea markets—multiple sellers, usually in an outdoor setting on weekends. Sellers usually pay a fee to set up; buyers sometimes are charged an admission fee.

Everybody Has a Garage Sale Story

You Never Know Who'll Stop By

Several years ago, a new black Porsche stopped in front of my house during my lawn sale. The driver was interested in the 1940s floor model radio that stood near the curb. After a brief discussion, he made an offer, which I declined. Then Christian Laettner, at that time a member of the Minnesota Timberwolves basketball team, got back in his car and drove away.

The "Call 911" Lawn Sale

On October 12, 1991, a beautiful autumn day, I decided to have a lawn sale in my front yard with my friends David and Stefan helping me. Everything started off well. Sales were brisk. By noon we were swamped with people. David was helping me outside and I asked him to go inside and get Stefan to help us.

David went in and I waited for him to return. He didn't. Finally, I went in to find them. I discovered David trying to revive Stefan, age 22, who had collapsed in my entryway. Stefan had evidently hit his head when he fell and there was blood on the carpeting and tile. David had called 911 when he found Stefan. I yelled to my customers in the front yard asking if anyone knew CPR. Two people responded. A fire engine soon arrived followed by an ambulance.

Meanwhile I had about thirty shoppers in my yard wondering what was going on. My wonderful neighbors took over the operation of the sale for me. The paramedics worked on Stefan for quite a while it seemed, and then rushed him to the hospital. A few hours later I learned Stefan had died. The autopsy said he died of cardiomyopathy, a hidden heart defect that pretty much killed him instantly. One of my vivid memories from that day occurred when I was later counting the money from the sale; thinking how meaningless the cash was in light of what had happened.

My Mom, Age Seven

What are the odds of finding a childhood photo of your mother at an estate sale? It happened to me in 1996. There was an estate sale at the house next to where my mother grew up. It was the last day of the sale and very little was left. I went up to the unfinished attic to look around and found a few boxes containing books. At the bottom of a box, something caught my eye. It was the back of a photo, about two inches high and about an inch wide. I picked it up and recognized it as a photo of my mother as a child taken in a Woolworth's photo booth. She had evidently given it to the

My mother, age 7

neighbors when she lived there in the 1930s. Somehow it survived all those years in a box in the attic while the ownership of the house changed. And what is amazing to me is that I happened to see such a small photo, the only photo in the box, and happened to turn it over. That's what I like about sales—the treasure you can find at the bottom of a box!

The Vase No One Wanted

The neighbors of my parents were going to have a garage sale and asked me to look things over to see if they had priced things right. One item that got my attention was a beautiful blue glass vase about eighteen inches high. It was in perfect shape, had no cracks or chips—and no identity as to who had made it. They had it priced at one dollar. I asked about it and they

63

said it was a wedding present they received in 1961. I said it might be valuable and to price it at least at $25, which they did. During their sale, they had some interest in it, but it never sold. After the sale they said I could have anything I wanted. The leftovers were all headed for Goodwill. I took the vase and a few other things. I had a friend get the vase appraised. It was worth about $75. I later sold it for $60 at a flea market.

Finding the Twin

As long as I can remember, my grandmother had a distinctive green lamp in her front window. My guess is that it was from the 1930s or 1940s. After she passed away, it became mine. Recently, I unexpectedly found its twin at the last day of a sale, half price. It's smaller than the original, but the exact same style. Makes me wonder if there is still another version out there somewhere in Garage Sale Land. You never know. This is how collections are born.

Sure, It Works Great!

After you go to a large number of garage sales, I think it makes you more of a skeptic and you begin to take the words of sellers with a grain of salt. A case in point was the time I purchased a color television at a garage sale. The seller said it worked fine, and maybe it was even operating when I looked at it. What he failed to say was that it was a fire hazard because you could only shut it off if you unplugged it. It went out with my trash the next day.

Answered Prayer?

Several years ago I went on a crucifix search. As a writer of spiritual meditations, I wanted a crucifix for my office, even though I am not Catholic. I looked at sales and flea markets and discovered the ones I liked were fifteen dollars and up. I didn't want one bad enough to pay those prices, so I continued to look. A few days later I was at an estate sale. It was messy and disorganized with things tossed all over. I went downstairs, walked into a room, and on the floor next to my feet was an old metal crucifix. It was just what I wanted. And the price was heavenly. The tag read 50 cents.

Against All Odds

During the late 1980s I purchased a Canon 35mm

camera that always took perfect photographs. Even my friends commented on the excellent picture quality. I took it on trips and got a lot of use out of it. In 2004, however, my mother dropped it on cement, and it broke. That was the end of it, I thought. I was without a camera. A week later, however, I was attending a neighborhood lawn sale. I was kind of rushing through it because there were so many sales and so much to see. At one sale, however, I walked right up to a table, looked down, and saw the exact Canon model camera, new, in the case, with instructions, for five dollars. What are the odds of that happening? I bought the camera, it works perfect, and I still can't believe it!

Snipe Hunting

Every year there is a neighborhood sale I attend and it has some sellers who are a "must" to visit each year. One of the sellers has a house at the edge of the

neighborhood and they always have a garage packed with interesting items. I always end up buying something from them. My most recent purchase was an old plate that had a painting of a bird on it. The plate was nine inches in diameter with gold trim and without any flaws. It was only one dollar, so I bought it.

Weeks later, I decided to use the Internet to research the value and history of it. The artist, R.K. Beck, had signed the plate. Another clue was it contained the Taylor, Smith & Taylor back stamp on the reverse. My Internet hunt revealed that the bird depicted was a "Common Snipe" and the plate was transfer printed about 1915. The artist had created several game bird plates. One dealer was selling the snipe plate for $65. That's what I call a profitable hunting expedition!

The Bicycle Thief

I was driving through an inner city neighborhood that was having their annual garage sale days when I saw an angry man chasing a young man on a bicycle. The guy had stolen the new bike from his yard and was riding off with it. The owner was losing his foot race against the bicyclist, so I pulled my car over and offered to give chase. He got in and the pursuit went on for several blocks. As we rounded a corner, we lost sight of the bicyclist. A block farther down, however, another motorist who had also witnessed the theft used her car to knock the thief off the bike. The thief left the bike in the street and disappeared between some houses. A bystander remarked that the guy would probably think twice before he ever tried to steal a bike again. You don't mess with garage sale people!

Real Good Luck

My father's birthday was coming up and I wanted to buy him a nice gift. My search took me to Garage  Sale Land where I found what I thought was the perfect gift. It was a glass art rendering of an Indian maiden. The artist was L. Goddard. It looked like a new reproduction of an old painting. I picked it up off the table and the seller asked if I knew anything about the item. An odd question, I thought. I replied that my father liked early Americana and this would make a great gift. I paid three dollars for it and took it home. My friend, David, stopped by later that day and happened to look at it. I was shocked when he told me the art piece was quite old, valuable and was actually an advertising giveaway. He showed me the words in the corner, "A token of good luck from Gadow Milling Company, Phone 10, Barton, Wisconsin." Yes, it was indeed a matter of very good luck for me!

The Map

This item was one of my first flea market finds and it has been hanging in my living room for decades. A local drive-in theater, now long gone, hosted a flea market on Sunday mornings. I went there and found this 1926 Election Map of Saint Paul, Minnesota, and I had to have it. It is a three-color street map of the city showing the 12 wards. The glass is hand blown and it measures thirty inches by thirty-five inches. I think I paid around ten dollars for it. It's still a favorite of mine.

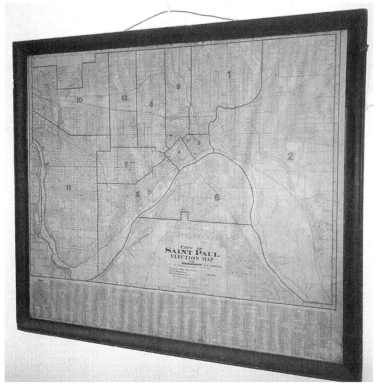

1926 Election Map

GARAGE SALE *fever!*

Thorton or Waldorf?

Years ago I came across a diary, which I still have, that was written in 1912 by an unknown south Minneapolis woman, evidently living near Lake of the Isles. Her entries were mostly from January through June of that year. She wrote about her upper class life, carriage rides around the lakes, and attending various concerts and plays. Well known local names like Dayton are mentioned. The diary also provided a glimpse into her love life. She was in love with a young man named Thorton and another man, Waldorf, and couldn't choose between them. I probably paid fifty cents to a dollar for the diary at a garage sale, a bargain for a personal and entertaining glimpse of a young lady's life so many years ago.

A Dusty, Dirty Vase in a Garage

It was an estate sale and the seller had packed the garage with all sorts of stuff. His prices were low and I purchased a few things, left, then decided to go back to take a second look. I was glad I did. High up on a shelf was an old vase that evidently had been there for years. Dusting it off, it was a distinctive Catalina vase, yellow on the outside, dark red inside. Perfect shape. No chips or cracks; it just needed a cleaning. He sold it to me for fifty cents. I enjoyed it in my home for many years before selling it for $40 at one of my lawn sales.

The Golden Boy

It was one of those impulsive buys that you are later glad that you made. I was at a flea market where this man was unloading a truck of vintage collectibles that looked liked they came out of an old mansion. The object of my attention was a 26 by 30-inch gold, ornate-framed photograph of a young boy standing next to a chair. It was quite heavy and maybe from the 1920s or 1930s. I had it in my hand as soon as it left the truck. It was just twenty bucks. It has been hanging in my living room now for over twenty years.

The VCR with a Surprise!

You see a lot of used VCRs at lawn and garage sales. Most are broken or the owners "don't know" if it works. Buying a VCR at a sale is always a gamble, but I got one that contained a surprise. I stopped at a sale where two young college-age women were selling lots of stuff, many items they said they were selling for their grandmother. Well, I started looking at granny's

VCR. It looked to be in good shape. They said it worked great and that she rarely used it. The price was right, so I bought it and they said they would put the money aside for the grandmother. They said granny would be pleased it was getting a good home. (There was a bit of overkill with the granny talk.) Anyway, I got it home and guess what—I could not get it to work. Finally I discovered the problem, a tape was stuck inside. So, I pressed the "play" button and yes, the VCR did work. The image on the television screen was of a naked man and woman on a diving board. Evidently, granny (or someone) liked porn flicks.

My First Radio

Collections are often like eating potato chips. You have one and then can't stop yourself. My collection of vintage radios began with a 1930s tombstone-style Admiral radio. It was a

case of being at the right place at the right time. The seller had just placed it on his front lawn and I got to it first ahead of several others. I was told it came from his lake cabin and the price was five dollars. The radio still works and was the first of over 100 vintage radios I purchased in the following years. Sometimes, one is not enough.

The Globe Lamp

I clearly remember buying it. It was a garage sale near my church. It was late in the afternoon and I wasn't expecting any huge finds. The garage was dimly lit and way in the back in the corner there was what appeared to be an old black globe of the world. The seller said it was actually an old lamp. Although it looked like metal, the globe/map was glass with a light inside. There was an on/off switch at the base. It looked like it was made in the 1940s or 1950s. She wanted five dollars for it, but assured me it was probably worth a lot more. I bought it, took it home, and found a place for it in my office where it stayed for years. Eventually, I looked it up on eBay and found a similar one selling for $250. Since I didn't want to risk damaging or breaking it at a yard sale or a flea market, I ended up putting it on consignment at an antique shop. Six months later, a collector made an offer of $200 for it, which I accepted.

Bagging the Birds

One of my favorite sales is a bag sale. It sometimes occurs at the end of an estate sale when the owner wants the house emptied of all unsold items. Buyers are given a large grocery bag and fill it with whatever

items are left in the house. You then pay the seller two to five dollars for everything you have in the bag. The house having this sale was in a bad part of town and I hesitated to stop, but I did. It was the third day of the sale, the final hours, and a lot of stuff was left. My big find was face down in the corner of the bedroom floor. It was a vintage ceramic table clock with two blue parakeets as decorative art. The bottom of the clock has the word "Holland," and on the clock face it reads, "Made in Germany." The clock doesn't work, but looks great on my bedroom shelf. It is the best thing I ever stuffed into a bag.

As Seen on TV

In the summer of 1994, I did something that resulted in having several local television stations cover my lawn sale. It was at a time when the national

Powerball jackpot first reached the $100 million mark. My idea was to give away a Powerball ticket with each $10 purchase of rummage. I called the local media and told them what I was doing. Reporters showed up to interview me and I found myself on the evening news on several stations. My neighbors were gone for the day, but saw me on television at their lake cabin. The "$100 Million Dollar Lawn Sale" banner across my front lawn was big news that day.

Bewitched!

During the 1950s, I remember each Halloween my mother would bring out a dark red witch candle about eight inches high and display it in our front window. She never lit it, to my knowledge, and I don't know whatever became of it.
Forty-some years later I was at an estate sale where everything was in boxes and scattered throughout the house. It was mostly junk from the 1980s and early 1990s. It was not promising. However, after digging through one box, what should I find? An orange, eight-inch witch candle

from the 1940s or 1950s. It was in mint condition, never used. The bottom of it had the words Gurley Candles and the original price, 89 cents. It was not the same as the one my mother had, but similar. As nothing was priced, I had no idea how much they wanted for it, but I knew it was worth about $25. I took it to the cashier's table and was charged 25 cents for it. I place it in my front window every Halloween.

The Peacock Lamp

I bought it on eBay. It looked great in the photo and the price was right. When it arrived at my house, however, reality set in. The white porcelain lamp shaped like a peacock was about eighteen inches high, made in the 1970s or 1980s. The manufacturer was unknown. It had a light bulb within the detachable base. The lamp was covered with bright beads of many colors that dazzled when the lamp was lit in a dark room. A few beads were missing, and I noticed a slight crack. The main problem, however, was that I had no place to put it. So, it became a mainstay of my lawn sales. Each year I would bring it out, people would look at it (never an offer, even) and then I'd pack it up and store it in a closet until the next sale. After doing this routine for a while a small miracle occurred and an older woman found it attractive and had to have it. I paid $11.25 for it plus $8.75 postage. I had it for sale for $15. She offered $10 and it was sold. Again, I was reminded, everything sells eventually.

Anniversary Plate

You see a lot of plates at sales and flea markets that celebrate anniversaries for businesses, churches and civic organizations. Many have calendars on them and serve as birth year plates. I own one of those. (These make great gifts if you know the year a friend or relative was born). I am amazed at how many plates are from out of state. The plates are usually quite cheap as the demand is not strong here for a Zion Lutheran Church anniversary plate from Lincoln, Nebraska. But that doesn't keep people from trying to sell them. A few years ago at an estate sale, I did find an anniversary plate I had to own. It was a 40-year anniversary plate for the church I attend, issued in 1975. I had never seen one before, nor have I seen one since at any sale. It now hangs in my kitchen.

Humpty Dumpty Doll

You never know what you will find in a box of stuff at a garage sale or an estate sale. One memorable find for me was a large stuffed handmade knit Humpty

Dumpty doll, probably from the 1930s. Whoever made it put a lot of work into it. It was light green with other colors. Humpty Dumpty had fallen into a junk box when I found it. It showed some wear, but was in decent shape. I paid ten cents for it and Humpty Dumpty now sits inside a glass display case in my living room.

One Last Story

Years ago, I was at a yard sale packed with everything imaginable. The prices were embarrassingly low. And the sale had just started. As a collector of vintage radios, I grabbed several table models and proceeded to the checkout line. I mentioned to the seller that I collected radios and that these were nice ones. He responded by inviting me inside his house and showing me dozens of radios, most of which he was not selling. His father was an avid radio guy. They were in the early process of liquidating the family home of 50 years.

We talked. I found out he was a seminary student. I had just had my first book published, a book of devotions, so we talked about that. I had a copy of the book in my car and gave it to him. He sold me a few more radios from inside the home and gave me several non-working ones. One of the radios I purchased was a rare FADA in mint condition. I paid $25 for it. It is now worth well over three hundred dollars.

As I was leaving, he told me that eventually they would have an estate sale to clear out the house. He asked for my telephone number and said he would call me.

About a year later, he called. The house had been sold and they were going to have an estate sale. He invited me over in advance of the sale and gave me my choice of anything I wanted to buy at his still embarrassingly low prices. I purchased or was given over one dozen vintage radios. (I still have all, but one). I also received some great antiques. I loaded up my car and he loaded up his van. Both he and his son helped me move the radios and antiques into my living room. On the day of the sale, he gave me an ornate 1929 Eveready floor model radio he had forgotten about. We sneaked it out of the house, past the house filled with buyers.

I have never forgotten his kindness or his generosity.

(Prior to the estate sale, I did warn him that his prices were way too low. He said he knew it, but the sale was not about making money. It was about finding new homes for family possessions).

My point in telling you this story is to convey the value of getting to know those people you meet on your garage sale journeys. There are many wonderful people out there, like the man in this story, who will go out of their way for you if you get to know them. Share your interests. Ask about interesting items you see at sales. You never know where a conversation will lead.

Questions & Answers

Question:

I live at the end of a dead-end street. When I have a garage sale, I advertise it in the local newspaper and put signs out. The problem is that my neighbors farther up the street see that I am having a sale and then set up their own sales. My potential customers stop at their sales and never make it to mine. Any suggestions?

Answer:

There are several things you can do. One might be some signs with arrows saying, "The biggest sale is straight ahead—keep going" and attach a balloon to each sign for added attention. You could also create some flyers that give your address and list what you have for sale. Give them to your down-the-street competitors and ask them to hand them out to those who stop. Another idea is to instigate a neighborhood sale. Get a bunch of homeowners to agree to a specific day, share the cost of an ad, then create a map of the neighborhood listing garage sale sites and what they have. The incentive is that neighborhood sales generate much more traffic than individual sales.

Question:

I have several hundred old 78 rpm records from my parents' estate and want to sell them. How much are they worth?

Answer:

Without researching the value of each, a rule of thumb is about $1 per record if they are in decent shape. That's what people sell them for at flea markets. You could ask more, or give a discount for volume purchases. Realize that your buyers will be collectors, not the average garage saler. Most will be interested in specific artists and some may want specific record labels. Be sure to remove all records that are chipped and cracked. They won't sell. If you have the thicker Edison label records, they could be priced at $5 each. You can also take them to a record dealer, but they will not give you as much and usually will not want all of them. If you do want to do some research, look up vintage records on the Internet for price guidelines. Some 78s are valuable to collectors. Another idea is to run a classified ad in your local newspaper to attract collectors.

Questions and Answers

Question:

When is the best time to have a garage sale?

Answer:

Early spring and late fall are the best times, although you can have them any time of year, except during winter if it snows in your state. In Minnesota, garage sale season usually begins in late April or early May and ends in October. Avoid having sales on holidays when people are busy or leave town. Usually sales are on Thursday, Friday or Saturday, often two or more of those days. Start about 8 a.m or 9 a.m and end about 5 pm

Question:

When there are multiple garage sales going on in my neighborhood, how can I get my sale to stand out from the others?

Answer:

What attracts people to garage sales is seeing lots of people looking over lots of stuff covering a lawn or driveway. I think if you can cover your lawn or driveway with items, you will attract a crowd and buyers. Spread your items out all over, on blankets, tables and in boxes. Give the appearance you have much to sell. If you don't have a lot to sell, invite your neighbors to move their stuff on to your lawn or driveway. Just ask that they price each item and put their name or initials on the price tag for you to keep track. Banners and balloons are good ways to draw attention to your sale. If you have some wood furniture, put that out. It is always popular and attracts customers.

Question:

Should I advertise my garage sale in the local paper?

Answer:

If you live on or near a busy street that has a high volume of traffic, you might want to skip the ad. If, however, you have something specific or large you want to sell, like a refrigerator or a dining room table set, an ad in the paper that mentions the item might increase your chances of selling it. Some people read garage sale ads looking for specific items. If you live on a quiet street or at the end of a dead end road that sees little traffic, I would definitely run the ad.

Question:

How can I get the best deals at a garage sale?

Answer:

Get to the sale just as it opens or while they are setting up, for best selection. On the flip side, many people get bargains at the end of the sale when the buyer will discount items greatly or listen to offers, rather than pack the stuff away and keep it. Also, feel free to make an offer on something you want. Cut a few dollars off the sticker price and ask. One technique

I have found effective, and it has been used on me, is to hold out a handful of cash and say "Will you take $25 for this?" It is usually easier for the seller to accept rather than reject a handful of cash.

Question:

You always see lots of books at garage sales at various prices. How do you price a book?

Answer:

At my sales, I price older hard covers (from the 1970s thru the 1990s) at fifty cents and paperbacks at twenty-five cents. Again, if the objective of your sale is to raise money, your prices should be higher. If you just want to get rid of books, the cheaper the better. Books from the 1920s and 1930s can be offered at five dollars each, but often I will see them for one dollar each. They are usually difficult to sell. Paperbacks by some writers, like Louis Lamour, generally sell for one or two dollars each. If a book is new, offer it for twenty or thirty percent of the original price—or what you feel it might be worth to someone. If there are no takers, lower the price later in the sale.

Question:

Can you sell old magazines?

Answer:

The great thing about garage sales is that you can sell anything, even old magazines. Magazines that seem to sell well deal with home restoration, gardening, and home improvement and design. Price them at 25 to 50 cents each. Older magazines from the 1920s thru the 1970s are often sought after for their advertising. People cut out the vintage ads and frame them. These magazines should be priced from one to ten dollars each, depending on age and condition. Some people also buy a magazine as a gift for someone based on the year of birth—a 1937 magazine might be given as a gift to someone born in that year.

Question:

What is the oddest thing you ever bought at a garage sale?

Answer:

I purchased an oak church pulpit and used it for many years as a plant stand.

Question:

Is it worth looking in the free box at garage sales?

Answer:

Yes, you will be amazed by what gets tossed in there. One time I found a complete 1920s bingo set along with some books from the early 1900s. At the conclusion of my sales, I generally create a large free pile near the street of things I don't want, things that didn't sell, or things I don't want to pack away and keep. Many people do this. It is a better alternative than hauling it to the trash bin.

Question:
Any tips on preventing shoplifting? How big a problem is it?

Answer:
I would put small valuables in a glass case with a note to please ask for assistance. I would also never leave the money box unattended. The only thing I ever had shoplifted from one of my sales (that I know of) was a new watch that was in a silver metal box. I went in the house for a minute and when I came back, the box was there and the watch was gone. Fortunately, the watch only looked expensive. I think I paid a few bucks for it. Generally I do not see shoplifting as a problem. The vast majority of people are honest. Still, keep your eyes open.

Question:
What type of things do people collect that I might sell at my sale?

Answer:
People collect just about everything. Collectors search for old fishing lures, railroad memorabilia, old dolls, bicentennial items, cook books, calendars (pre-1970), old coins, knives, radios, old or historical newspapers (pre-1960), cameras, baseball cards, beer cans, key chains, postcards, and kitchen collectibles,

just to name a few. Often people will tell you what they collect and ask if you have it for sale.

Question:

If something is broken, can I try to sell it anyway?

Answer:

You can try to sell it, but price it cheap or maybe offer it for free. Very few people want broken clocks, phones, radios, cameras, VCRs, televisions, chairs, computers, and so on. If something is broken, put a tag on it saying so.

Question:

Is there any market for typewriters?

Answer:

A manual or even a working electric typewriter has little value, although you have a better chance of selling an electric one. Price them five to ten dollars. Don't bother trying to sell a broken one or one with missing letters. The old black models from the 1920s might sell for ten dollars and up, mostly for use as an office decoration. Writers like to have them around. And there are a few typewriter collectors.

Quick Reference Guides

Garage Sale Ingredients

To have a garage sale you need…
1. Start-up money, so you can give proper change. Get one dollar and five dollar bills and several dollars in quarters. About $25 in total is usually enough.
2. Bags and newspapers for wrapping items.
3. Merchandise to sell. The more, the better. Quality counts!
4. Advertising. Signs, banners, newspaper ads, balloons.
5. Tables for displaying merchandise. Large empty boxes (face down) can also be used as mini-tables.
6. Blankets. Open blankets or rugs on your lawn can display books or other items.
7. Scissors / tape / paper / pencils / extra price tags.
8. Good weather (good luck!).
9. Several people to help run your sale.
10. Check-out table for cashier with calculator or scratch paper to total up sales.

Top 10 Garage Sale Mistakes Made by Sellers

1. Pricing your items too high.
2. Having too few items to attract any interest.
3. Holding a sale in a poor location without any advertising.
4. Not greeting and chatting with your customers.
5. Not cleaning up items prior to the sale.
6. Not putting a price tag on each item.
7. Leaving signs up all over town after the sale is over.
8. Trying to sell broken items that belong in the trash.
9. Poor displaying of merchandise, under tables, in boxes, and so on.
10. Forgetting to thank the customer for making a purchase.

Quick List for Promoting Your Sale

- Signs on street corners
- Classified ad in daily newspaper
- Classified ad in weekly newspaper
- Sign on a telephone pole
- Small ad / notice on bulletin board at local store
- Notice on bulletin board where you work
- Notice on bulletin board at church
- Tell your neighbors and let them tell others
- Put a sign on top of your parked car
- Attach balloons to your signs
- Send out some e-mails
- Put something that generates attention on your front lawn

Seller's Checklist

Getting Ready to Have a Sale

- ❑ Date(s) of sale:
- ❑ Set-up time:
- ❑ Starting time:
- ❑ Ending time:
- ❑ Price stickers
- ❑ Price all items
- ❑ Clean all items
- ❑ Advertising / signs done
- ❑ Start-up change obtained
- ❑ Enough tables for displays
- ❑ Tape / scissors / paper
- ❑ Bags / wrapping paper
- ❑ Plenty of help
- ❑ Electrical items tested
- ❑ Check-out table ready
- ❑ New batteries in non-electrical items
- ❑ All signs removed when sale is over

Ideas to Increase Sales

1. Lower some prices on items you really want to sell toward the end of your sale.
2. Group items of the same price together. Have a 25-cent table or dollar table. You can also offer a discount for multiple purchases. For example, buy one item for 25 cents or five items for a dollar.
3. Got a lot of inexpensive items? Have a sale where every item costs one dollar. Promote this with large signs.
4. Have a special promotion. For example, one free paperback with any purchase.
5. If someone is looking at an item for a while, go over and talk to him or her. Ask if they have any questions. Gently close the sale; maybe knock a bit off the price. Be a salesperson!
6. The 50% off Sale. Have a table where all items are half off the sticker price.

Buyer's Checklist

Getting Ready to Attend Sales

- ❏ Time you want to start:
- ❏ Route planned?
- ❏ Garage sale ads circled?
- ❏ Money to spend
- ❏ City / neighborhood maps
- ❏ Umbrella
- ❏ Paper / pen / notebook
- ❏ Reference / pricing guides in car
- ❏ Dressed for the weather?

How to Price Items

Pricing is important as it can make or break your garage sale. It requires careful consideration, often some research, and should not be rushed. Use input from others. Price your items before, not during, your sale.

Before you set prices, decide if you are selling items to raise money or if you are having a sale just to get rid of stuff. Price your items accordingly.

All items should have a price sticker.

Would you like to walk into a retail store (or an antiques store) and find out that none of the items are priced? Be considerate of your customers. If an item is not priced, a customer may be interested, but not enough to ask you about it. When items are not priced, the customer may assume you want a high price for it, when in reality your price may be very low. They might set it down and walk away. Pricing starts the selling process. And you are not constantly asked, "How much is this?"

Do research.

Attend garage sales and flea markets. Keep an eye open for items similar to what you want to sell. Take notes. See what others are asking.

Inexpensive items sell best.

At my sales, items priced at 25 cents, 50 cents, and one dollar sell the best. As prices increase, selling chances decrease.

Antiques & collectibles

If an item is older than 1965, price it carefully as it may be a collectible. However, just because something is old does not make it valuable. Again, research is a must. Visit some antique stores in your area or a flea market and look for similar items. Look up the item on the Internet. Ask a friend who is knowledgeable. If you are still unsure, ask for a customer's best offer. By the way, a garage sale is not always the best way to sell antiques. A flea market, a classified newspaper ad or the Internet may be a better choice. You may need a larger base of prospects to find that specific collector who wants your item.

Leave room for bargaining.

Many people may not want to pay your asking price and will make an offer instead, usually on items priced five dollars and up. In order to compensate for this, you may want to add 50 cents or a few dollars to the item so that you have room to bargain. If in doubt on a price, price it higher rather than lower. You can always go lower or take an offer. If you are open to offers on some items, post a sign saying so.

Rough guidelines on common garage sale items.

Check out other sales in your area so that your prices are competitive. Price according to condition and how new it is, about 10 to 25 percent of original cost. Items should be clean; electronics should be working.

Paperbacks: $0.25 - $1
Hardcovers: $1 - $3
CDs: $1 - $6
DVDs: $3 - $8
LPs: $0.50 - $1
Videotapes: $2 - $5
Color TV sets: $10 - $25
Black & white TV sets: $5
VCRs: $5 - $15
Clocks: $1 - $3
Radios: $1 - $5
CD player: $10 - $15
DVD player: $ 15 & up
Lamps: $2 - $20

Power tools: 25% of cost
Single glasses: $0.25 - 0.75
Bicycles (older): $5 - $15
Microwave: $5 - $10
Games/puzzles: $1 or $2
Children's clothing:
$0.25 - $3
Picture frames: $0.25 - $2
Furniture: 20% of cost
Pans: $1 - $2
Sweatshirts: $1 - $2
Telephones: $2 - $10
Framed art: $2 - $10
Stuffed animals: $0.25 - $5